curiousabout
LIZARDS

BY ALISSA THIELGES

AMICUS

What are you

curious about?

CHAPTER THREE

3

Lizard Care
PAGE
14

Curious About is published by Amicus
P.O. Box 227
Mankato, MN 56002
www.amicuspublishing.us

Editor: Rebecca Glaser
Series Designer: Kathleen Petelinsek
Book Designer: Aubrey Harper
Photo Researchers: Alissa Thielges and Omay Ayres

Library of Congress Cataloging-in-Publication Data
Names: Thielges, Alissa, 1995– author.
Title: Curious about lizards / by Alissa Thielges.
Description: Mankato, Minnesota : Amicus,
[2023] | Series: Curious about
pets | Audience: Ages 6–9 | Audience: Grades
2–3 | Summary: "Nine questions
that kids would ask and well-researched, easy-to-understand
answers teach readers about life with these reptiles,
including terrarium needs, handling techniques, and lizard
behaviors like head bobbing and arm waving.
Simple infographics support visual learning. A Stay Curious!
feature encourages kids to keep asking questions and
models media literacy skills. Includes table of contents,
glossary, and index."—Provided by publisher.
Identifiers: LCCN 2021060256 (print) |
LCCN 2021060257 (ebook) |
ISBN 9781645493082 (hardcover) |
ISBN 9781681528328 (paperback) |
ISBN 9781645493969 (ebook)
Subjects: LCSH: Lizards as pets–Juvenile literature.
Classification: LCC SF459.L5 T45 2023 (print)
| LCC SF459.L5 (ebook) |
DDC 639.3/95–dc23/eng/20220119
LC record available at https://lccn.loc.gov/2021060256
LC ebook record available at https://lccn.loc.gov/2021060257

Photo credits: Alamy/Juniors Bildarchiv GmbH 11, Vladislav
Bagnyuk 16–17; Dreamstime/Amador García Sarduy 10,
Tkatsai 15; iStock/ApuuliWorld 8–9, boschettophotography
15, Captainflash 15, DikkyOesin 6, Ekaterina Aleshinskaya
12–13, NagyDodo 18–19, tpzijl 15, Warmlight 7, Xesai 7;
Shutterstock/Elena Schweitzer 15, Irina oxilixo Danilova 7,
Kuttelvaserova Stuchelova cover, 1, ivespots 2, 4–5, 13, Sebastian
Janicki 3, 15, MarekZatko 21, mlorenz 7, Steve Bower 7

CHAPTER ONE

What is the biggest pet lizard you could get?

A black-throated monitor lizard can be a good pet for experienced owners.

A monitor lizard. They are very big. The black-throated monitor grows up to 7 feet (2.1 m) long! Iguanas are the next biggest. Green iguanas can grow to 6.5 feet (2 m). These big lizards are not for beginners. They need a lot of space.

DID YOU KNOW?
The Komodo dragon is the largest lizard. It is more than 10 feet (3 m) long! It is not a pet.

What's a good pet lizard for beginners?

A bearded dragon makes a good pet.

Bearded dragons are popular. They are easy to care for. People like these lizards' spiny beards. These **reptiles** are friendly. They will hang out in your lap. Their medium size makes them easy to hold. They can grow 2 feet (0.6 m) long and live 10 years.

CHINESE WATER DRAGON
UP TO 3 FEET (0.9 M)
10–15 YEARS

LEOPARD GECKO
UP TO 10 INCHES (25.4 CM)
15–20 YEARS

GREEN ANOLE
UP TO 8 INCHES (20.3 CM)
4–8 YEARS

GREEN IGUANA
UP TO 6.5 FEET (2 M)
10–15 YEARS

CRESTED GECKO
UP TO 9 INCHES (23 CM)
15–20 YEARS

CHAPTER TWO

Why does my lizard bob its head?

A leopard gecko does push-ups to show how strong it is.

DID YOU KNOW?

Lizards can do push-ups.
It shows their strength.
It means, "This is my land."

This is a show of **dominance**. A fast bob is a challenge. It means, "I'm the boss." A second lizard might slowly nod back. It's saying, "Yes, you are the boss." A pet lizard might greet you with a slow nod. It knows you are in charge.

A green iguana is a good climber.

My lizard is waving at me. What does it mean?

This cute behavior doesn't mean "Hello." Your lizard is showing that it sees you. In the wild, this stops a sneak attack. It means "I'm watching you. Don't try anything." Waving could also be **submission**. The lizard is saying, "I'm no threat!"

A bearded dragon's wave could be a sign of stress.

Why do lizards lie under a heat lamp?

It is warm. Lizards are **cold-blooded**. Their body temperature is the same as their environment. They need a heat lamp to stay warm. They also need a special **UV light**. It helps them create vitamin D. Lizards need this vitamin to stay healthy.

An iguana stays warm under a heat lamp.

CHAPTER THREE

What do you feed a pet lizard?

It depends on the type of lizard. Geckos and anoles eat insects. They are fed crickets and worms. Iguanas only eat plants. They eat leafy greens and fruit. Bearded dragons eat both insects and plants.

A water dragon eats live insects.

LIZARD FOOD

Worms

Insects

Fruits and leafy greens

Does my lizard need a bath?

A leopard gecko
cannot swim.

No. Lizards don't need to be washed. But they soak in water. This helps them shed. Lizards shed in patches. The pieces flake off better when wet. Just make sure the water isn't deep. You wouldn't want your lizard to drown!

DID YOU KNOW?
A leopard gecko sheds every 4 to 8 weeks.

Can I take my
lizard on a walk?

An iguana can be trained to walk on a leash.

Yes! In the summer, large lizards can walk outside. You need a leash and a special harness. You don't want your pet to wiggle away! Walking is great exercise. Small lizards should stay indoors. But they

Do lizards like toys?

Yes. Toys keep your lizard happy and active. Think simple. A new tunnel or cave are great. A bearded dragon may push a small ball around. Lizards can play outside their **terrarium**. Just make sure they can't sneak away.

A lizard may enjoy playing outside if it's warm.

DID YOU KNOW?
Some bearded dragons like to watch TV.

ASK MORE QUESTIONS

How do you set up a lizard terrarium?

How do lizards hear?

Try a BIG QUESTION: What kind of lizard would be best for me?

SEARCH FOR ANSWERS

Search the library catalog or the Internet.
A librarian, teacher, or parent can help you.

Using Keywords
Find the looking glass.

Keywords are the most important words in your question.

?

If you want to know about:

- how a lizard terrarium is set up, type: LIZARD TERRARIUM SETUP

- how lizards hear, type: LIZARD HEARING

FIND GOOD SOURCES

Here are some good, safe sources you can use in your research.
Your librarian can help you find more.

Books
Geckos
by Kate Riggs, 2023.

Lizards
by Derek Zobel, 2021.

Internet Sites
**Nat Geo Kids:
Bearded Dragons and Other Reptiles**
*https://kids.nationalgeographic.com/
videos/topics/wild-pets-at-the-vet*
Nat Geo is a good source for learning about animals. Watch this video for tips about owning exotic pets.

What Reptile Should I Get?
*www.thesprucepets.com/
choosing-a-pet-reptile-1239401*
The Spruce Pets publishes articles about pets. They are reviewed by veterinarians.

Every effort has been made to ensure that these websites are appropriate for children. However, because of the nature of the Internet, it is impossible to guarantee that these sites will remain active indefinitely or that their contents will not be altered.

SHARE AND TAKE ACTION

Check out lizards in a zoo.

Look for reptiles at the park.
You might find small lizards, frogs, or turtles. You can watch, but don't take them home. Wild animals should not be pets.

Be safe around lizards.
Learn their behavior and know when it is okay to play with them.

GLOSSARY

cold-blooded To have a body temperature that changes based on the temperature of the surrounding area.

dominance The state of being more important or powerful than others.

reptile An animal that is cold-blooded, lays eggs, and is covered in scales.

submission The act of accepting the authority of someone else.

terrarium A glass or plastic box used to create a living space for small land animals.

UV light Ultraviolet light. Light that can't be seen by the human eye. It is given off by the sun.

INDEX

About the Author

Alissa Thielges is a writer and editor in southern Minnesota who hopes to inspire kids to stay curious about their interests. She doesn't own any pets but would love to have a turtle and dog someday.